Snoozing in a Hurricane

by Averett Jones

Illustrated by
Ben Lansing

Rural Legends
Volume 1

Hermes
Publications

Hermes Publications
P.O. 849
490 Railroad Ave.
Keysville, VA 23947
434-736-0152
books@southsidemessenger.com

ISBN: 978-0-9791460-0-8

Dedication

Dedicated to my parents, Mrs. J and The Chief, who know what real love is.

The Chief's love for Mrs. J is evident every time one of his sons picks wildflowers for their love. We witnessed true love as Mrs J. walked the Chief through his long illness and to the end. We see true love every day as we watch Mrs. J patiently wait until she is rejoined with The Chief for eternity.

When Susan and I were married they accepted her and love her as one of their own. They were perfect parents who raised at least one imperfect child. In spite of all of their efforts, they still loved and encouraged me as I climbed "Fool's Hill." They never made excuses for me when I was wrong, but still stood beside me as I suffered the consequences for my actions.

They held a continual open house for all of our friends and always made everyone welcome.

Mrs J. and The Chief never discouraged us from attempting any project because we might fail. Thanks to them we all have spread our wings and flown to unexpected destinations.

Thanks for Everything, We Love You

About the Author

Averett is 51 years old and has been married for 20 years to Management, who was originally Susan Kathleen Mitchell. Susan is 41 and is a delivery driver for UPS. They live in rural Southside Virginia and have 3 children.

He is a graduate of SVCC, was an English/Speech major at Longwood College, and has a Masters in Guidance and Counseling from Longwood. He taught school for one semester and spent 3 years as a Rehabilitation Counselor before giving up on traditional employment. Since then, he has been a commercial beekeeper, goat farmer, house painter, bee exterminator, and has operated a sawmill, ditch digger and well-boring machine. He went to Russia in 1996 with his family and worked at an orphanage for several weeks.

In 2004 he helped start a new local newspaper, *The Southside Messenger*, and finally started letting other people read his writing. Averett claims to come from at least three generations of frustrated writers and says if he doesn't write and get the stuff out of his head then his head will explode.

He began reading before starting school and still claims to be behind on his reading. His favorite author is Mark Twain, his favorite food is very rare beef, his favorite beverage is coffee, his favorite car is a 1940 Plymouth Pickup, and his favorite hobby (excluding Management) is laughing at himself, people in general, and the absurdities of life.

About the Illustrator

Ben Lansing is a cartoonist, illustrator, writer, and teacher. Born in Richmond in 1983, Ben grew up in Southside Virginia where he developed a love for art and a unique, creative sense of humor. In 1999, Ben began work as a cartoonist for the Petersburg Progress Index and the Richmond Times-Dispatch. Ben attended Richard Bland College of the College of William and Mary and completed degrees in business and history at the University of Richmond, where he graduated with honors in 2005. Ben's advertising business, Lansing Advertising, offers innovative, humorous illustrations and cartoons for business advertising. Ben's national award-winning cartoon panel, Out of Order, is currently published in newspapers across the state of Virginia, including *The Southside Messenger*. Ben is also the author and illustrator of Bigwigs of Classical Music, an illustrated history of classical music, and the editor and illustrator of Turning the Tide Online (tttblog.com), a web site that encourages young adults to live for Christ in a self-focused world.

Visit Ben's web site at www.benlansing.com

Averett, Management And A Boring Life

Averett has lived a typical boring life absolutely devoid of excitement. Management, also known as Susan and his wife of 20 years, will confirm this. HOWEVER, it is her opinion that, as Averett's wife, she is the little girl holding onto the string of a large kite which is constantly being blown in various directions and that her excitement comes from attempting to control the kite. Her other theory is that Averett is the eye of a hurricane and that although his life may be peaceful, everyone around him gets caught in the path of destruction.

Born in 1955, Averett received, at the age of 2 minutes, the first of many spankings. This event occurred in the Alamance County Hospital in North Carolina. This also apparently started not only regular spankings but also regular trips to various hospitals to repair damage to his anatomy usually caused by poor judgment.

At the age of 6 years, he developed rheumatic fever, which was treated at the time (and possibly still is) by allowing no vigorous exercise or excitement, and with weekly trips to a hospital for tests. This had a profound effect on the young boy's psyche. According to numerous undocumented sources, (i.e. his parents, siblings and relatives), the young lad spent the next fifteen or twenty years attempting to recapture the year of missing excitement.

Bypassing the 2nd grade, Averett now found himself with two missing years for which he required compensation.

Upon moving to rural Southside Virginia at age 9, he found rural life offered enhanced opportunities for potential excitement and for adding to his growing collection of scars and injuries.

In addition to falling from trees, being bitten by dogs, and getting hit by cars like city children, rural children fall from horses and cows, cut themselves with axes and knives, fall from barns and silos, are bitten by snakes, skinny dip in ponds without lifeguards and fall through ice on ponds. The only opportunity enjoyed by city children which is unavailable to rural youth is being mugged in a subway.

Living on a farm also allowed him a growing collection of native Virginia fauna. These were usually NOT pets. Pets are creatures with which you can have a mutually beneficial relationship. A horse that bites, kicks, occasionally throws and stomps the human, is NOT a pet. A cat that attacks not only dogs but also all humans is not a pet. It is more like a miniature Genghis Khan in a fur coat.

The sick fox that wandered into the yard and fainted was not a pet. After three days of dedicated nursing, the fox died. Averett realized the fox had no further use for its skin and proceeded to remove it, planning to tan the hide. In an event known as vulpine (fox) revenge, Averett was infected with Tularemia. This is not a kind disease. He had strong suspicions that he might die from Tularemia. These suspicions were verified when he overheard the doctor telling his mother, "It will all be over in a week."

Although surprised by survival, Averett realized life was short and that he was now two years and two weeks behind on excitement.

As a teenager, Averett discovered he had a certain charisma that attracted police, ambulances and school administrators.

Upon graduating from high school by "the skin of his teeth," several institutions of higher education requested that he not return. He currently holds three or four college degrees but is unsure how or why they were presented to him.

After several narrow escapes, Averett finally died at the age of 22 from a reaction to bee stings but was "jump started," and given a second, second chance.

Currently 3 years, 7 months, 3 days, and 22 minutes behind, Averett continues to live a boring and peaceful existence with the hurricane raging around him.

Averett has been an unpublished and ignored writer for 30 years. He hopes you enjoy his Rural Legends which he wrote in order to see something of his in print other than the tips of his fingers at the police station.

Baseball, Moms and Apple Pie

When he was 12, the son asked if he could join the Dixie Youth baseball team. I have never played baseball and although I think it is fairly silly to stand still while someone hurls a hard object at you while you attempt to deflect it with a stick, I encouraged him to try. Competition is good, and learning to win graciously and to lose with dignity are good lessons for life. Most importantly, at the rate evolution is apparently reversing itself, the ability to use a club may be a useful job skill later in life.

So I was at my very first baseball game wishing Aaron Doubleday had been hit in the head with a projectile or a club and had never invented this game. On the other hand maybe he was and this game is the result of the injury. The excitement is so thick you could cut it with a bat.

I was reading a Wilbur Smith book and wondering if God is using this as punishment for some of the sins of my misspent youth. I quickly developed a survival plan. If I heard wood hit leather or whatever it is, then I looked up. If the ball was going in the general direction of the son, I continued to look, and if not I continued to read.

I made my first observation about baseball (hereafter called BB) parents very quickly. They stutter in sentences while using a child's name for punctuation. "Eye on the ball, John, eye on the ball." "Good cut, Bill, good cut." I am a fast learner so when the son strikes out I said, "I'm proud of you, son, I'm proud of you. You did your best."

Next, one of our players is called safe at right base. They kept telling me it is first base, but I haven't been out of the dating world so long that they can pull that one over on me.

The next batter hit the ball to the fence. The kid at middle base missed the catch and they told me the batter is going to run home. I'm was not sure why he was running home, but it sounded like a good idea to me.

I began to learn how this game works. The batter stands at the plate. Another kid throws the ball at him and he attempts to hit it. It is very simple: three strikes and you are out. Then again, sometimes it is a strike even if he doesn't strike at it and sometimes it is a ball and if he gets four of them he can walk to right base. Sounds pretty simple to me. Just put four balls in your pocket and walk to right base.

The next batter is hit in the head with the ball and falls to the ground. The umpire says he can walk but they carry him to that little English basement thing they sit in. This is beginning to get a little confusing.

The next batter hit the ball high in the air. The announcer shouted, "It's a popped fly-------and--------he's out." I was so embarrassed for the poor child. I pretended to read my book. Half of the parents cheer, the other half look dejected. No one helped the poor child repair his fly. I knew those funny looking pants wouldn't hold up.

I am now at my second game. Parents are still stuttering in sentences. Some are shouting orders to the players from the stands. Children, as usual, are ignoring their parents. Parents are angry at being ignored. My son gets walked to right base and tagged out at middle base. "I'm proud of you son, I'm proud of you." Another child's father embarrasses him so much he walks home rather than ride with dad. "You struck out, Dad, You struck out."

It is the last game of the season; the Son says he isn't going to play next year. Darn! Then he gets a good hit and makes it to left base; the other parents say he made a triple.

I don't know where he made it, but he knows better than that. I intend to have a long talk with him about alcohol after the game. He didn't learn it from me; I never touch the stuff.

The season is over. I thank the Coaches, "See you next year... maybe."

What? Practice tomorrow night? Playoffs start Wednesday!!! I think I'll reconsider that triple.

Plymouth Pickups, Flat Tires and Store Boughten Beer

When I was in high school, I fell in love. It wasn't one of those silly temporary childish romances. This was the real thing. I will have to admit the object of my affections was 15 years older than I and had right many miles on her, but she was beautiful. I saw her one day as I was going work. I knew then and there: if I had to wait the rest of my life, some day she would be mine.

You should understand that this in no way interfered with those silly temporary childish romances that were part of my training for marriage later in life.

Unfortunately, we never know they are silly and temporary until they are over.

Clementine had curves you just wouldn't believe. She was small and black, except for the rusty places, and had the sexiest grill I have ever seen on a pickup truck.

For the next six months, I stopped by every Friday to chat with her owner. Each week he would tell me how he bought her in 1954 and had never driven her. He would then tell me there were only six thousand 1940 Plymouth pickups ever made and that she was not only beautiful, but she was also rare and expensive.

At the time, it was frustrating, but at least I got to see the object of my affections. This early training was of great benefit later in life. Now that I am the father of a daughter, it is even more important. I think to myself, "This young bum isn't interested in talking to me. He just wants my Plymouth Pickup."

In any case, one day as I was visiting Clementine, her owner was sitting on his porch drinking home brew. If you have never had the dubious honor of being offered home-made beer brewed from potatoes, take my advice and decline. There may be worse beverages but I have never encountered them and I hope I never do.

On a positive note, the home brew was an icebreaker and we finally started working on a deal. We started out discussing a thousand dollars and finally agreed on twenty-five dollars, two recapped tires and a store boughten beer.

I have always thought he didn't care about the money or the tires; he just wanted to get the taste of spoiled potatoes out of his mouth. I wish I had asked for his recipe. A thing like that could come in handy.

We towed Clementine home without any problems other than four flat tires and the fire. We would have had more flats but we ran out of tires and the fire was only a small one and it went out as soon as it burned what was left of the wooden bed.

Clementine has been a patient lady and has been faithfully waiting as I bought, sold, wrecked and junked several hundred other cars.

Like my bride Management, who knows she is the only woman in the world, Clementine knows she is the only truck for me.

Southerners, Yankees and Taxes

I was recently asked if I were born "nawth" of the Mason-Dixon line.

I beg your pardon, Suh. I was born in Carolina and grew up in ***South***side Virginia. My father was from ***South*** Carolina and my mother is from ***Southern*** Alabama. Our original Jones came to ***South*** Carolina from ***Southern*** Wales. I am an American first and also a Southerner. We have a different perspective on the "War between the States." We are NOT still fighting the war, nor do we wish the United States of America were two separate countries, but "The War" is a real and personal part of our history.

As a child, I played on numerous Civil War battlefields. We were taught the history, knew the Generals by name and shot fireworks from the cannons. The North, on the other hand, has few Civil War battlefields and also was the location of the massive immigrations from Europe after the war. These immigrants added much to the North but of course didn't have this heritage to pass to their children. We are well aware that the historical fact is that the North won the Civil War. We just don't choose to discuss that. I have often proposed this motto for the South: "The Southern States of America, Gallant in Victory, Arrogant in Defeat."

Years ago, when passing through a small town in Ohio, we stopped to visit a Civil War Monument in a courthouse square. The inscription was, "Dedicated to the boys in blue who fought in the war of the rebellion." We attracted a small crowd as my companion proceeded to "educate" the Yankees on states' rights. Several very nice "boys in blue" arrived and offered to give us food and lodging for the duration of the war. We politely declined.

They then insisted that we allow them to escort us to the town limits, which we accepted. I wish I could remember the name of the town because they invited us to come back for a visit any time in the next century.

Many Southern residents with Northern heritage think that when a Southerner calls them a Yankee they mean it as an insult. This is NOT true and we do not consider being called a Rebel to be offensive.

If you are from nawth of the Mason-Dixon line, you are a Yankee. We really don't mean it as an insult. In the South there are three classes of people with northern heritage: Yankee, a Northerner who is still in the North or who comes to the South, spends money and leaves; DamnYankee (one word) is a Northerner who stays and adapts to Southern lifestyles; Damn Yankee is a Northerner who moves to the South and spends the rest of his or her life telling locals what we are doing wrong.

Listen closely for the space between the words. The space means you have been insulted. Yankees in the South are easy to identify, even the ones who have taken voice lessons and learned to slur their words. All you do is mention taxes. Any Yankee can and will tell you to the penny how much his taxes were back home.

There is only one way to be a Southerner. You must be born in the South to Southern parents. Although it is possible to be born in the South to one Southern parent and be Southern, it is not if both parents are from the North. I did not make these rules; so don't blame them on me. The Southern attitude is: "If your cat has kittens in the oven they are not muffins."

One of my distant ancestors came from the North and stayed. We prefer not to discuss this issue. I have a friend who was born in the North but his mother was from Carolina. He could almost pass for Southern except that he actually believes the Northern Propaganda he was taught as a child. He thinks the North won the Great War.

I have attempted to explain that when a country loses a war, then the winners stay and take over. Apparently his childhood brainwashing makes it impossible for him to understand this simple fact. I even took him to Sailor's Creek Battlefield and showed him the route of the so-called "Lee's Retreat." What kind of retreat meanders through the countryside for several weeks? You've never seen running until you have seen a Southern boy with something chasing him.

This is simple proof that Lee took a leisurely stroll to Appomattox where he said, "If you'll leave, we'll let you say you won."

My buddy can't get away from his brainwashing, but I'm sticking to the Southern facts.

Well Pumps, Lightning and Rose

It was a typical day in Southside a few years ago. I received a "No water" call first thing in the morning. The pump had been hit by lightning and there was extensive (and expensive) damage.

It was a typical job. We had to pull the pump that was 200 feet deep and the lightning had made the pipe brittle so it kept breaking and splashing us, which, on a hot day, was no problem. When we finally got the pump to the surface, there was a large black ball on the bottom.

Now I had pulled hundreds of pumps and had never seen one like this. The customer was standing there and asked what it was. I said, "I don't know" and touched it and it EXPLODED and sprayed us with hot oil.

The customer asked, very calmly, "Why did you do that?" I thought about saying, "Many electricians don't know that this is the fastest way to dismantle and check a pump," but I was too busy wiping hot oil from my body and there was no water (remember the pump is bad) to wash it off.

The customer told us when we arrived that she was slightly short in the cash department. Since my motto is cash, checks, negotiable securities and live chickens, I ended up "buying" a car, a fiberglass replica on a Volkswagen running gear. The car is as cute as it can be, long and low with lots of chrome and a pervertable top, or is that a contortable top?

It's cute and Management (my bride) is cute so they will look great together. It needs lots of work (Management is in pretty good shape) and I used to be pretty good on VW's when I was a teen. How can I resist? We got it running and decided to drive it the 5 miles home. The first mile was great.

Then it stopped.

We cleaned out the gas tank (which was full of water) and got it running again. This time we made it 50 feet. In the 70's, Slim (my teenage VW mechanic alter-ego) could keep a VW limping along forever but now that I needed him again he was lost in the deep dark recesses of my mind.

Slim is apparently very satisfied being lost in the 70's but he surfaced long enough to remind me that VW carburetors are famous for sticking when they have been sitting for years. I hit the carb with a wrench and, sure enough, Slim was right and we made it another 100 feet. We spent the next hour hitting the carb and driving until it stuck again. Hitting the carb and driving, hitting the carb and driving.... I hope there isn't a new law against car abuse.

There is always a bright side to everything. Since we didn't have any brakes (which Slim said we didn't really need anyway) it was probably safer this way. You know, looking back, Slim didn't always use the best judgment. We made it home, rebuilt the carb and gave the car to Management for a 4th of July present.

She loved it but asked if it ran. Why is it that the first question everyone always asks me about a new vehicle acquisition is "does it run?" She then jumped in and drove off to show a friend. It probably would have been wiser for her to ask about the brakes but we aren't going to discuss that. Why don't people ask the questions that are important? All I intend to say about this is that, "It has no Bra-a-a-a-a-a-aa-a-a-a-a-k-e-s" drifting down the driveway is one of the most frightening phrases I've ever heard.

The car survived and Management survived. I even survived but it was questionable for a while.

Slim, the son, and the Godfather fixed the brakes and Management and I went for a drive. This is a cool little car!

Management named the car Rose after the comic strip lady who transforms from a Mom to a Biker Babe. Should I be worried about this? Will Management leave me and drive her cool car to Vegas? Why would a beautiful lady in a neat car want a middle-aged, dull and boring husband? Not a problem! She can't leave me. She needs Slim to keep the car going!

I've never driven a car like this. It's kind of neat. People wave at the car and smile. Anything that makes people happy just has to be good. This brings me to another of Slim's errors in judgment. I've always said it doesn't matter what kind of car I drive, and when I was single I said that any woman who cared what I drove needed to date someone else's car.

I had no idea the attention people get with neat cars.

Maybe my life wouldn't be so drab, dull and ordinary if I'd had one of these as a kid. My motto was calico cars and tri-color trucks. Three colors are good. This one has brown fenders, cream body and beige top so it's still a calico—just a socially acceptable calico. I really can't see the difference between this and my VW with one red and one green fender. Three colors are three colors. Management says there is a difference, so it must be so. I never question the judgment of the woman who chose me.

Management and I decided to drive to Charlotte Court House and show her car to her parents. We leave town, the top is off, the wind is in our hair, people are smiling and WE ARE COOL. I've never been cool before; this is interesting. Then the carburetor sticks again. I get out the wrench, hit the carb, drive a bit, hit the carb...

You lose a lot of cool points sitting on the shoulder of the road in a cool car in 99-degree heat. You lose even more points when everyone can see that you are hitting your engine with a wrench. I hope they don't think I'm having a tantrum. Management says you don't have to lose cool points, and picks up her cell phone every time we stop. Now, that's really cool, sitting on the side of the road in a cool car safely talking on your phone.

So now we are cool again, but still not making progress. An hour later we have traveled eight miles. I clean the carb and we start back home. I decided to take the short cut that will bypass the two steep hills on the way. As we pass a big mean dog, I make the observation that this is not a good car for bad dogs.

The car accepts the challenge and we coast to a stop in front of a huge "BEWARE OF DOG" sign. The first thing that comes to my mind is, "This is not cool."

There are at least 12 large mean dogs in the yard.

Fortunately there is a chain link fence higher than the car between them and us. Then I realize, higher than the car is only four feet tall and the dogs can look over the top and down on us. The dogs apparently don't appreciate "Cool."

They are looking at us like we are dinner and the car is a chew toy. They are not impressed with the cell phone. We discuss making a run for it and letting the dogs bury the car. Apparently the vibration from the barking and snarling shook the trash in the carb loose, the car starts and we're off!

The dogs are disappointed. It only takes an hour and a half for the eight miles home. We stopped five times in the last mile, to make phone calls of course, and all of our neighbors stopped to help. You know, Slim was right, I just don't have what it takes to be cool.

More Mumble, Idiots and Big Shots

This week I celebrated the 49th anniversary of my birth. This means I have just entered my 50th year of existence. I had planned on writing on how this event would change my life. I intended to complain more about the government, kids, and social programs. I had planned to talk more about the "Good Old Days" and how much harder life was then. I was looking forward to being on one of those "fixed incomes" in 15 more years. This "broken income" is beginning to become a bit tiring. Yes, I had big plans until I remembered I was forced to come to terms with "Old Age" at the tender young age of 40.

It happened like this. Management and I went to dinner to celebrate the 40th anniversary of my birth. We had a nice dinner and Management was teasing me about not knowing how to dance. I have dancing down to a science. I stand on the dance floor and watch her dance. Imagine my amazement when an attractive young lady grabbed my hand and said, "I'll show you how to dance." She then said, "Move like I just did." I responded, "If I move like that, my behind will fall off." I was beginning to get a little concerned. Why is this attractive young lady acting like we are old friends? Then it came to me. I was once her baby sitter. At that point, I bypassed middle age and came to terms with old age.

I found a new Southside Mumble this week. "*Weben marred fi yah.*" Usually in Southside, *fi-yah* is when a combustible material is ignited. A *Fi yah* is also called a far. On the other hand if you are terminated from your job, then you have been *fard*. *Weben marred fi yah* translates into Standard English as "We have been married five years."

Last week, I received several interesting phone calls. One accused me of being a "Big Shot." I was beginning to take offense when I realized I deserved it. When we started the Messenger, I went shopping and bought two brand new tee shirts. I apologize to all for showing off. My favorite call was a message left on the answering machine. The caller said that I was an idiot and several other names I am not putting into print. He then offered to inflict bodily damage upon my person.

Now, I have been called all of the names numerous times in the past 49 years and there is evidence that at least some of them are accurate. An idiot is a person with an IQ of below 25. I don't recall taking the test but who am I to disagree. The thing that concerns me the most is that the caller is apparently of lower intelligence than I. At least I have more sense than to leave a threatening message on a recording. Between the two of us we are drastically lowering the Collective Intelligence of Southside. Sorry about that.

The next call accused me of slashing tires. That's right, slashing tires. I must be having one of those Jekyll and Hyde episodes. I have stashed tires, my van has clashing tires, I have slashed wires, I have even flashed at fires but I have absolutely no recall of ever slashing a tire. I called the police and reported the incident. I hope I'm innocent; I would hate to become a vandal at almost 50.

Middle School, Detention and Three Licks a Day

Our Editor just assigned me to write "How I Spent My Summer Vacation."

Well Editor, it was just another typical summer. Eight of us got together and started a newspaper. It is fun. The end.

I always hated those assignments. Many of my former teachers (and current friends) will tell you I have been on permanent vacation all of my life. Makes it tough to decide where to begin.

My in-school vacations began in the 9th grade. The Supreme Court had just ruled that "separate but equal" schools for whites and blacks were unconstitutional. Randolph-Henry High and Central High had merged and we attended Middle School at the old Central High building. Most of the students didn't have a problem but due to the drastic changes and the merging of two schools and two faculties, the administration was somewhat unsettled.

This presented fascinating opportunities for social research. I discovered that if you can convince a teacher that you are incapable of doing the work, they would give passing grades for "trying." This was a satisfactory situation for first semester. Then Mrs. Lindsay checked my standardized test scores and that vacation was over. Oh well, it was fun while it lasted.

These were the days when corporal punishment was still permitted in school. None of us had ever heard of child abuse. We would receive demerits for any infraction of the rules. Three demerits resulted in one day in detention during lunch. Detentions could be traded for one lick with a large wooden paddle wielded by a sadistic administrator. There was a maximum of three licks allowed at one time. I always assumed this was so the administrator wouldn't get tired. Do the math here. This meant I could get 9 demerits a day, trade them for licks and still get to lunch. It was a win-win situation. The Sadist got to spank me; I could do anything I wanted and still avoid detention. Another interesting item for those of us waiting for licks was that we had to watch the others get theirs. This presented an interesting dilemma. Was it better to be at the front or rear of the line? Would the Sadist be tired or warmed up at the end?

One day there were four of us waiting, and at the first lick two of them backed to the door. Before the third was administered, they were back in detention hall. Unlike me, they could learn by example. I'm certain both of them have accomplished great things in life.

Near the end of the year I made a mistake. I neglected to "do the math" and exceeded the demerits I could trade. I was in detention and getting my three licks a day. I completed Central Middle School still owing them 53 days in detention. I hope the records have been lost. I'd hate for them to come collect them now.

Old Friends, Black Cats and Skeletons in My Closet

I must be getting more popular. Today I was accused of having a Vendetta and skeletons in my closet.

The Vendetta is apparently a fancy Italian sports car that I most certainly do not have and I just checked every closet in our house. No skeletons.

Well, no human ones anyway. There was one mouse that must have gotten into the supply of poison Management was saving for me if I fail to get the junk cars out of the yard, but that was an unintentional victim. Then I realized they were making fun of several of my former girlfriends. The ladies in question were certainly slim but it is rude to call them skeletons. Besides, that was over 20 years ago and has nothing to do with The Messenger.

I was just informed that a "skeleton" is something from my past that I am hiding. That's another story. I have lots of skeletons. There is an 1858 savings bond that I hid ten years ago and still can't find. Ditto, a City of Portsmouth dollar bill which is still lost. Lots of stuff is missing in action around here.

When the daughter was about 8 years old, she discovered a box of pictures in my office. She brought them out and asked who they were. "Just old friends of your dad," I said. "This one is pretty, who is she?" "She's a girl I dated before I met your mom." Well, that 8 year old was ready to scratch eyes. "I guess she is pretty, in a homely sort of way," she said, "but mom is prettier." A wise man knows when not to talk.

Then we were looking at my mom's photo album. Interestingly, there was a hole cut into every photograph directly beside me. This validates two cosmic truths. First, there was a hole in my life prior to Management AND that women from eight to eighty stick together. I was again corrected. A skeleton is something ugly from my past that I am hiding.

I can confess to that also. I have had several ugly friends. So what's the big deal? Some of you are pretty, some of us are ugly. Life is like that.

More correction. It appears that to be a legitimate skeleton, it must involve the police. Yes, I have skeletons. Many years ago, Southside Virginia was very poor. Keysville had a midnight curfew. I always thought it was to save on candles and lamp oil. Our local policemen must have been poorly paid and couldn't afford watches. I would be sitting on the curb and an officer would stop and ask if I knew what time it was. I never did and the kind officers would give me a ride home. I always appreciated the ride since I lived several miles from town and because the local Judge had borrowed my driver's license. See what I mean about a poor town?

The police cars must have been purchased without speedometers since they would often stop me and ask me how fast I was driving. Come to think of it, that was just before the Judge borrowed my license.

Our local police were a laid-back bunch of guys. I only saw one policeman excited in all of my teen years. We were driving through Farmville on Main Street. I was in the passenger seat when I noticed someone had dropped a pack of Black Cat firecrackers in the floor.

Realizing immediately that possession of fireworks was illegal in Virginia, and choosing to litter rather than possess illegal fireworks, I tossed them out of the window. This is where the skeleton comes in.

Somehow, the fuse to the pack was exposed and touched the end of my cigarette just prior to leaving the car. The fireworks slid to the curb and exploded just as any "black cats" would. The noise volume was quite satisfactory. The buildings created a "valley" which echoed and reverberated for some time.

And that should have been the end of the story. But there is more. The noise volume was intensified by the chance occurrence that a car was parked at the curb directly above the fireworks. The gentleman sitting in the car created additional volume. Unfortunately for me, the gentleman also happened to be employed by the Farmville Police Department. I suppose the flashing red lights on top of his car should have been an indication of his employment. In any case, I remember the officer as a very excited man with a red face, a loud voice, and what appeared to be a nervous twitch. He took us down to his office and introduced us to several other people. They gave us an appointment to see the same nice Judge who had my driver's license. The officer then promised to "skin me alive" if he ever saw me with fireworks again.

In today's world, such a promise would constitute police brutality and would have fractured my developing self-esteem. Then, as evidenced by my current "whole skin," I developed a permanent aversion to any fireworks in the proximity of officers of the law.

Sorry, I'm out of space. The rest of my skeletons will have to wait in the closet.

Snakes, Purses and Criminals

A friend and I bought an old pickup to sell the parts on eBay. When we first looked at the truck, there was a small black rat snake living in the glove box. I consider this to be an asset. I like snakes. Snakes eat mice and mice chew up things.

My friend has a somewhat different opinion of them. He isn't normally a nervous person but he is watching the truck carefully. I hope it (the snake) doesn't surprise him when he is under the truck. He will probably turn it over. The truck, not the snake.

Snakes have gotten a bad rap since the Garden of Eden. I have met many people who still hold a grudge over the Eve thing. They say God told us to kill snakes. The exact quote is, "You will bruise his head," not, "You will chop him to itty bitty pieces." Besides, it was Satan who tempted Eve, not the serpent. The serpent was just another victim and has had to pay the price for his involvement ever since.

If the snake shows up under the truck while he is working on it, my friend will have a bruised head, not to mention any damage to the truck. Then he will have to go to confession for getting it backwards.

I like snakes, but I have to confess when I was twelve I did a terrible thing. I still feel guilty about it.

It was a hot August day in Southside Virginia. We had exhausted our usual entertainment options when I found a huge Black Racer. Racers do not make good pets. They are fast and irritable and when you get them hot they are faster and more irritable. In short they aren't much fun on a hot day.

I took him into the barn to let him go so he could eat rats and be irritable alone, when we noticed one of my Mother's old purses. It happened to be just the right size to contain five feet of black racer with just enough room for him to be irritable. Well one thing led to another and shortly thereafter we were hiding in the honeysuckle on the side of Hwy 40, watching the purse on the shoulder of the road.

Every car that noticed the purse slowed down and we assumed they thought "some woman left her purse on the top of her car and it fell off." I was disappointed in the quality of the passersby. No "good Samaritans" in this crowd. Then an older car with five or six people in it drove by. They slowed down, turned around and drove slowly by going the other way and looked carefully. They turned around again and drove slowly by the purse. We are laughing. They will open the purse and get a surprise. We will catch the snake and do it again. The door opens and one guy leans out, snags the purse and they accelerate quickly. They must be snake lovers also but they are stealing our snake.

Just as the car is shifted into third gear, it is all over the road. I've never seen a car with that much power. I'm impressed. I was disappointed in the quality of the car. You have seen and heard cars with huge radio speakers that rhythmically bulge in beat with the music. Well this one was bulging, but certainly didn't have any rhythm. It was sort of like popcorn. Then the driver's door flew open and he abandoned ship. First appearances were deceiving. It wasn't the driver, it was the passenger who had crawled across the driver and exited.

Even at the young age of twelve I would have recommended not jumping from a moving car and if I felt the need to jump, to do it on the grassy side of the road. The remaining passengers were exiting the rear windows. This was an early lesson in lifeboat mentality. Had they made an orderly exit, it would have only taken seconds to clear the car.

The two men trying to simultaneously exit the rear window were stuck. The driver must have gotten his first aid confused. It is drop and roll when you are on fire, and back away slowly when confronted by a wild animal. As he rolled down the highway, the car ran into the ditch.

The men were apparently criminals and we had just prevented a terrible crime. They were screaming about finding someone and killing him but wouldn't get near the car. So I hope their victim escaped. The terrified snake survived the accident and in good racer fashion raced into the woods. They must have really wanted the snake as they spent almost an hour searching the woods.

Their language was inappropriate for my tender twelve-year-old ears as were the things they were planning for their intended victim when they caught him. We never saw the snake or the criminals again.

I felt bad for days. Although we had prevented a murder by delaying the criminals, I had done a terrible thing. I resolved not only to never do it again but also to prevent others from doing the same.

So I ask you to make the same vow I did that day. Please repeat after me: I will NEVER frighten a snake with a person again.

Computers, Cookies and Email

I am getting about 50 emails a day now from people I don't know. My computer-literate child says it is because of the cookies in the computer. Well, that's certainly not my fault. I've spilled several cups of coffee on the keyboard but I never eat cookies. Besides, it seems to me that cookie crumbs in the computer would attract mice, not mail. There are five categories of messages that I receive.

Email #1: "Make more money, get rich quick." They all offer an easy way to make lots of money. I have several problems with this. Why is a guy who has made millions of dollars willing to share it with me? Most of the people I know with lots of cash not only want all they have and all they can get --they want mine also. These people obviously have missed the point or their cookies are crumbled. I can't work any less or I'd be unemployed. Where is one that offers "Drink Coffee and Make Money?"

Email #2: "Millions of women" the emails state, "want you." Want Me??? There is clearly a mistake here. Uncle Sam didn't even want me. Nobody but Management ever wanted me and she was too young to make an informed decision. One stated that thousands of women wanted my body. Well, I suspect my body would be an upgrade for the average 80 year old, but what's in it for me? I signed an organ donor card when I was 16 and they are welcome to my spare parts after my demise, but taking the whole thing, particularly NOW, is a bit much. On the other hand, if I respond to one of these ads, Management might be personally removing and selling some of my body parts.

Email #3: "Lose weight fast and easy." Again, BAD COOKIES. The one today offered to help me lose up to 200 pounds. If I lose 189 pounds I'd be back to my weight at conception. If I lose 200 pounds, I would not only cease to exist, I'd be a negative Averett- sort of a miniature black hole. Besides, my outlook is much too positive to become negative. This defies all laws of physics. A positive can't become a negative.

Email #4: This is my favorite. Mr. PAUL KHUMALO in South Africa wants my "KIND REPLY." He has heard what a wonderful honest upstanding man I am and wants my help "transferring" a gazillion dollars out of a government account. He is willing to swear that I am the heir to Mr. Bryan Smith. For my "kind" help he is willing to pay me 1.2 million dollars and some change.

First of all, when we are dealing with this much money, what kind of tightwad would worry about the change? Secondly, why would he be looking for an honest man to help him steal this money? I think he would have better success looking for a crook. I wrote him back that I was in reality Mr. Smith's heir and to please stop trying to steal my money and forward the entire balance to me. He never replied to my letter.

Email #5: This one really bugs me. I know they can keep track of lots of things I do via the computer but coming to my house and looking into my van is a little much. These emails state my equipment or tools are too small for the job and that for 29.99 they can upgrade them. Management isn't going to like this one any more than she liked the one on the women who want me. I already spend too much on tools. One states that I need a "bigger hammer." If they are going to poke around in my van, they need to get all of the information. If I wanted to do bigger jobs then I might need a bigger hammer. As I don't do any demolition work, I don't need a sledgehammer. A small hammer is fine for small jobs. Besides, what I really need is a new set of wrenches.

I think the only solution to the cookie problem is to put a mouse in the computer.

TV, Computers and Saving Time

We spent 6 hours last night saving time on the computer. I only wrote one paragraph in those six hours but computers always save time and who am I to argue? I won't even mention that I could have written that same paragraph in longhand in 6 minutes.

Our home became afflicted with a computer in 1996. I had successfully avoided owning a television and had intentions of avoiding computers also. Both remind me of a brooding one-eyed Easter Island statue which takes over both the décor and the usability of a room.

In '96 I needed some critical information from a friend in Russia and needed it immediately. Every time I called the conversation was identical. I do not speak Russian and no one except Sergei in his home spoke English. "Sergei please," I'd say. "Nyet Sergei, Nyet Fax, Click" was the response. At $3.78 a minute and no information, I was getting frustrated.

A friend suggested email. All I would need is a computer and an e-mail address. The friend loaned us the computer and I signed up for the free Juno email. At every attempt to log in, the same message appeared. "An unexpected character appeared and cannot be served." It was obvious that the computers knew what I think of them and not only resented my appearance but intended to punish me for my resistance.

After I spent many hours saving time, the friend convinced the computer to accept me. I have always suspected it required a sacrifice of some kind but no one will confess. The original computer was only useable for e-mail and games, which was a satisfactory situation to me. Once the Russian project was completed, Management (my bride) and the offspring began to lobby for a better computer.

"Just think of the time you can save," and "It will be great for research," and "We can use it for homework." I continued to resist. I am well aware that being an "information junkie" is one of my numerous character flaws. Management prevailed. We traded for a used, pre-dented computer that would do everything they wanted.

The one-eyed beast took up residence in our home and nothing has been the same since.

A computer requires accessories. First you must acquire a 12-year-old child if you don't have one. This is part of the operating system. A computer simply will not operate long-term unless a child occasionally sits in from of it, makes a few passes of his or her hands, taps a few keys and informs the adult how easy it is. Keep in mind this is done at almost the speed of light and the child either cannot or will not do it in slow motion or explain. This is part of appeasing the computer gods.

Step two is the actual computer. The child will speak in a language that makes Russian sound easy. It has 250 meg o ram, TLC motherboard, floppy disc, seedy rom, GTX capacity and lot of other un-translatable words. I suspect this chant is part of the process of making it work.

This brings us back to last night. My children have grown up and are in college and I have no one to intercede with the computer gods on my behalf. I suggested to Management that we create another technician. She not only declined to participate but also wisely observed that this would result in a delay of 12 years before becoming functional. She also noticed that the cost of divorce and remarriage on my part would negate any benefit from producing one without her assistance. This leaves me with the final option of taking the computer to a repair shop.

These shops are staffed with qualified professionals who are in reality 12-year-old children cleverly disguised as adults. They will intercede with the computer gods on my behalf and will sacrifice pictures of dead presidents and in no time the computer will be saving me time again.

Cable TV, Hedge Trimming and Take a Chicken to Lunch

It was brought to my attention that September is National Chicken Month. That's right, National Chicken Month. In honor of this auspicious occasion I intend to wear my chicken hat, and avoid all possible controversial topics this week.

It seems sacrilegious to even think about eating chicken in September; after all it IS their month. In researching this topic I found a presidential directive that states with a bunch of whereas, here fore to's and fanfare that America is obligated to celebrate this occasion. I envision parades of chickens, chicken flags, chicken politicians and chicken tenders. Whoops, scratch the tenders.

I also found that September is National Alcohol and Drug Addiction Recovery Month, Food Safety Education Month, National Preparedness Month, National Cholesterol Education Month (I intend to start educating my cholesterol as soon as I finish this), National Rice Month, (Condoleezza is moving up fast) National Sewing Month and National Honey Month.

September also has National Historically Black College Week, Farm Safety and Education Week, Invisible Chronic Illness Week, Singles Week, and Suicide Prevention Week, to name a few. The scary thing is that these lobbies and our politicians have spent thousands of hours and lots of money to achieve this. Why do chickens have a month and Black Colleges only have a week? Something is wrong here. When Chickens have more clout than Suicide Prevention, then we need an Abolish Self-serving Politicians Year. Marisa D'Vari has proposed a National Shameless Promotion Month, which will go nicely with National Be Kind to Editors and Writers Month, which is also celebrated in September. We're not even going to discuss Cable TV Month.

On another topic, several citizens are concerned that I let Management trim the hedge in front of our office. They seem to be concerned that I forced her to do this while I drank coffee. The idea of my forcing Management qualifies as the joke of the week. Management and I have different views of grass and shrubbery. I prefer grass and shrubs to have a wild natural look, much like my hair but without the bald spot. She prefers square shrubs with flattop haircuts and yards that look like little green armies with every soldier at attention. My solution to overenthusiastic grass is to open the gate to the goat lot and let the goats do their goat thing and reduce the height of everything. This does not suit Management who believes there is a correct and optimum height for every plant.

Early in our marriage I made the mistake of goat trimming the shrubs. I found the result to be aesthetically pleasing and there were no clippings to remove. An additional benefit was that the shrubs would take years before they needed trimming again. This was when I learned that there is not only a maximum shrubbery height but also a minimum one. Management takes a maternal interest in a shrub once she has trimmed it. There is sort of a cross-species bonding and anything I might do will interfere with this relationship.

I suspect the shrub relationship is related to housekeeping and cleaning. When children are young, everything we do self-destructs within minutes. A clean house is trashed: the sink is full of dishes and the hamper is again full of dirty clothes, that is, if you have children who are well trained enough to use a hamper. A meal that required minutes of slaving over a hot microwave is consumed in seconds leaving nothing but scraps and another load of dishes. The shrub on the other hand remains trimmed for weeks and never complains that it doesn't like the haircut. In any case, after the complaint I went out and offered to assist Management with shrub trimming. She chased me off with a power hedge trimmer. I almost spilt my coffee.

The Sun Shines, Birds Tweet And Hurricanes

Contrary to rumors started by those who know me, my world is always a peaceful place. Management says the best description of life with me is a little girl holding a big kite, which is constantly pulling her in different directions. As I make it a point not to disagree with the woman whose biggest decision was to marry me, I must accept that I am a kite.

However, from the kite's perspective, it is pretty peaceful up here. Floating around with the buzzards is nice and out of reach to all of the things going on down there. Another friend claims that although my life may be peaceful, I am the eye of a hurricane and that everything and everyone around me is dealing with the storm.

Another friend proposed the theory that I live in an alternate universe that is unaffected by the storms in this one. In any case, life is peaceful and serene here. The sun always shines, the birds always tweet and life is always good.

The first time I told Management the sun was shining in the midst of a storm, she was concerned. "It is raining," she said. Of course it was raining. I attempted to explain that although it was raining, the sun was still shining. This resulted in a long conversation during which she attempted to slip off and call the people with the white suits and big butterfly nets. I finally convinced her that unless there was an enormous cosmic light switch that turned off the sun when it rains and at night, then THE SUN ALWAYS SHINES. It is a matter of perception.

So, regardless of the eye of the hurricane, the kite, or alternative universe, my life is peaceful and dull. I decided this weekend to do something to add some excitement to my drab dull normal life.

First, I slept late. Then I got out of bed on the other side. I took a big chance and removed the "Do Not Remove under Penalty of Law" tag from my pillow. We sat on the front porch instead of the back and drank our coffee. I had mine black for the first time in 40 years. Whoa!

While we were drinking our coffee, the oak tree in the front yard fell and hit the lamppost. If it had been about 10 feet closer it could have been exciting. But it didn't and you just can't beat having a load of good firewood delivered to within 10 feet of the front door just as it is beginning to get cold.

We finished our coffee just as the storm ended. As I got up, I noticed a large wasp nest under the seat of my chair. Once again, I missed an opportunity for excitement.

Management immediately started asking where I had last misplaced my Epipen for bee sting allergies, which was unnecessary since I wasn't stung. This gives some proof to the eye of the hurricane theory. On the several occasions I passed out in Dr. Ailsworth's office after a bee sting, everyone was somewhat excited. I, on the other hand, was peacefully asleep.

Back to last Saturday. We went grocery shopping and started at the wrong end of the store and used the wrong side of the aisles. As I was leaving the store a long black stretch Hummer stopped at the door. The chauffeur was wearing a tuxedo and rolled out a red carpet to the door of Wal-Mart. He opened the rear door and out stepped... some guy in a cowboy hat. He said "Yehaw" several times and offered to sign autographs. After signing autographs on Wal-Mart receipts and two on children he got back in the limo and left for the airport. Who was that hatted and booted man? Everyone but me seemed to know and he didn't introduce himself. He might have been famous or he might have been someone just looking for some excitement.

Chickens, Hats and Absolute Fools

Where did I get the Chicken Hat? Management gave it to me. My father always said, "A gentleman wears a hat." It is probable that by "a hat" he meant a standard issue fedora type hat, but he wasn't specific. I maintain that if he had meant a specific type of hat he should have been more precise. My first hat was an old railroad type hat that one of my classmates gave me. Then as now, I always tried to dress in the latest fashion. I found the cap to be most suitable, and the green frog (who I named Horace) giving the peace sign was an added benefit. For more formal occasions I had a perversion of a gray top hat that looked like a cross between a top hat and a witches hat but was flat on top.

It made me look like a swishy leprechaun with a thyroid condition but such is the cost of being fashionable. That hat was lost in one of the skeleton type incidents that I don't intend to discuss. I replaced it with a black felt hat like the ones everyone who was not a cowboy wore in the westerns. That hat created lots of problems for me. For some reason everyone who saw it had a terrific urge to throw it to the ground and stomp on it.

Many could not resist the urge and did just that. I thought it was somewhat unreasonable to damage my personal property but as a 98 lb. weakling who didn't want to do the Charles Atlas thing, it seemed even more unreasonable for me to object. After a year, the hat was pretty tattered and I replaced it. In retrospect, some of the places I went while wearing the hat may have contributed to the problem, but I still think they could have removed it from my head before stomping on it.

For the next few years I wore a variety of standard issue hats. They just didn't happen to be standard issue for this area or the twentieth century.

Then there was a three-year period I didn't wear a hat. I somehow became employed in a white-collar professional type job. This job required suitable clothes and no hat. I even had to wear shoes. Although I enjoyed the job, I realized it was time to quit when one of my friends saw me in jeans and made the comment that I didn't look like myself. Who knows where I might be if I had not had the good sense to run: I might be successful.

For the next five years I was a beekeeper. This occupation requires a hat called a pith helmet. I was not going to put anything on my head called pith anything. It was during this phase that I met Management. At that time Management was working for me and was called the Leprechaun. Somehow, during the next three years her name kept changing. It went from The Leprechaun to Mrs. Beekeeper to Mother to Management.

Shortly after we were married she bought me a hat that I'd always wanted but could never find. I never stopped to wonder why she bought me a fool's hat. The next hat she bought me was a jester hat, I suppose for me to wear when I was feeling foolish but was not being an absolute fool. The third hat was a stocking hat with a two-foot long tassel with a bell on it. I loved that hat. When she bought it, the sales clerk commented that there wasn't a man in the country damfool enough to wear it. Management responded, "Mine is and he will love it." I wonder what she meant.

Fan Mail, Fire Trucks And Calendar Photos

I received a nice fan letter today. It said, "I always enjoy your Rural Legends. I go home, get on my knees and give thanks that I am married to a normal man. How did you convince Susan to marry you? Signed, Thankful."

Well, Thankful, it happened like this. She proposed and I said yes. I've always suspected she was after my snake collection. When we met I had the finest collection of Virginia snakes in the state, not to mention several baby snakes I brought back from Florida. I know they were babies because each one had a rattle. Grown snakes are much too macho to carry toys.

She did a great job of hiding her interest in my collection. I remember our first date. There was a beautiful eastern king snake crossing the road. I slid to a stop, dodged a few cars and trucks, and grabbed the snake. There was a logging truck coming so I jumped back into the car and handed her the snake. Well, I tried to hand the snake to her but she was 50 feet down the road and moving fast. See what I mean about concealing her interest?

After we were married, my snake collection mysteriously vanished. I've always suspected she has them hidden in a vault somewhere and goes to gloat over them, much like some art collectors. If she didn't marry me for the snakes it must have been because I promised to Love, Honor and Cherish her forever and that life would never be boring.

In the interest of being fair to me, I have to admit that Management does have a character flaw. She hates fire trucks. Once early in our marriage, in response to "What did you do today, honey?" I said, "I took the kids to school, drank four cups of coffee, fixed a well pump and two lights, bought a fire truck, picked up a paycheck, got the kids from school, cut the grass, and..." I was interrupted with "YOU BOUGHT A FIRE TRUCK?"

She didn't even hear about the rest of my day. See what I mean? The woman has issues with fire trucks. Other than that she is perfect in every way, which is why I love, honor, and cherish her and will never buy a fire truck again.

I received a phone call this morning that a camera crew was coming to Charlotte Court House to take a picture of a truck for a calendar. I can read between the lines here. A camera "crew" to take a picture of a truck? Heh Heh. You don't need a crew to take a picture of a truck. I've seen those calendars in every garage and shop I've ever been in. They take a truck or car and drape it with several attractive young ladies. It is clearly my responsibility to observe this crew and take pictures of them taking pictures.

I arrive in Charlotte Court House to find the truck and camera crew are now in Keysville. After returning to Keysville, I located the crew taking a picture of a truck. I've never seen anything like it. Several trucks filled with equipment, computers, cameras, screens to block the sun and a crew of 7. You won't believe what I saw. They were taking a picture of a truck. Just a truck and nothing but a truck. On the other hand, the crew was very nice, informative and interesting. I learned a lot about calendar photos.

But once again, no excitement in my dull normal boring life. I did manage to catch two copperhead snakes on the way home and snuck them into the house. I know Management will be excited when she finds them. It usually takes her about two days to hide them wherever she hid the others. I wonder why she never thanks me?

Junk, Demolition Derbies and Wooden Indians

I received a request that I write about my junk this week. I'd be more than happy to comply but I don't have any junk. I have several acres of antique, classic and parts cars tastefully sprinkled about our landscape and even more tastefully accessorized by local native flora concealing the lower portions.

These desirable antiques also provide homes and habitat for local native fauna. There is a popular local belief that if I cut my grass I would find a car. This is not true. "Find" implies I would locate something I don't know is there. I already know what I have and about where it is.

Amateurs might forget where a car is parked but professional collectors such as myself have a constant mental inventory of all cars by location, amount of damage and usability. I feel certain these rumors were caused by someone overhearing Management playfully threatening to put rat poison in my Cream of Wheat and preparing my obituary in advance of my demise.

Another persistent rumor is that our home looks like a messy Cracker Barrel restaurant. This is not true either. I was decorating with historic memorabilia with a patina of ferrous oxide long before there was such a place as a Cracker Barrel restaurant and long before I had Management for that matter. In any case Cracker Barrel looks like a neat version of our home not the other way around.

Shortly after we were married Management and I went to see a hypnotist. The next day I had a terrific urge to remove all of the junk from the house. The only problem was, we didn't have any junk. I carefully searched through all of my collectables and memorabilia and found no junk. I even checked the dictionary. Junk is "worthless material some of which may be reused" or "worn out and fit to be discarded" Nope, no junk in our house. I did have the urge to camp out in the back yard for a few days though.

We went to the Demolition Derby this weekend. A derby works like this. Six cars are put in a small parking lot surrounded by concrete walls. They run into each other until only one car is left running; sort of like rush hour on the expressway. Then the survivors of the six heats are put in together and the last one running wins.

I had two problems with this. One is that after the derby the losing cars looked better than the one we drive. Management agrees something should be done about this. I intend to see if any of the contestants want to trade.

My other problem is that the winning driver is one of the people who made fun of me for flying an ultra light airplane.

I fly safely and peacefully and have only had one real OOPs in two years. He just had several dozen crashes in as many minutes. I guess I'm better off with my dull, peaceful life. As we were leaving several people assumed we were contestants and clapped.

If I park on the side of the road, someone will invariably call 911 to report the accident. I meet more nice policemen and rescue squad personnel, but for some reason they always want me to walk down the line in the middle of the road or have the rescue squad take me to the hospital to be treated for head injuries.

Management just expressed an interest in a wooden cigar store Indian. This woman should have anything she wants but this Indian concerns me. What would we do with a wooden Indian? The only place we could put him is in front of the office where it would just stand there, looking attractive and doing nothing. With the exception of the attractive part, THAT'S MY JOB. Should I be worried?

Cell Phones, TV's and VCR's

Contrary to popular belief I am not opposed to progress. I intend to move into the 20th century as soon as possible. When Management suggested we get cell phones I was justifiably terrified. Cells are located in federal, state and local penal institutions and in monasteries. If I were planning on spending time in a cell I'd want a phone, but to the best of my knowledge, I don't have any cells planned in my immediate future. Does she know something she isn't telling me? I decide to play it cool. "Sure Honey, maybe we do need cell phones." She responds with, "It would be great for emergencies, keeping in touch and romance."

Let's take this one at a time. What kind of emergencies can you have in a cell? "My door won't open!!!!" "Brother Alphonse is breaking his vow of silence!!!!!"

Keeping in touch is good, but if I have to take a vow of silence, a phone won't be of much use. Tap once for yes, two for no. We aren't even going to discuss romance in a cell. Management explains what she means by a cell phone. I knew that. I was just kidding.

Cell phones are great for romance. I can call and say "Hello, Love, I miss you", at any time. And she can hear "Hello...I... you." It's great. A fill-in-the-blanks phone call. Right after getting the cell phones, we met for lunch one day. An hour later my romance phone rang. She said "Honey ... had.... beep beep scritch," followed by silence." I tried to return the call but was out of area.

My first thought was that she had had an accident. Then I filled in the blanks. "Honey, I had a nice time." I blissfully drove home to find a message on the answering machine. "Honey, I had an accident. I'm in the hospital." Maybe it isn't wise to mix romance and emergencies.

People have been encouraging us for years to get a television. I have seen televisions, I don't think they are going to catch on. Just another fad like hula-hoops. Why would anyone sit and watch pretend people doing pretend things? Why would they allow some of these people into their homes? If it is so great, why don't people on television watch television?

I had a sales visit from a satellite dish company. The nice salesman guaranteed me 77 channels with nothing else to buy. I told him if he could get me 77 channels with no additional equipment I would take it. We completed the contract and then I asked him where I would get the channels. He looked at me like I was stupid. "Duh, on your TV." As he was tearing up the contract he laughed, "Mr. Jones," he said, "Have you considered that a satellite dish would make a beautiful bird bath?"

Management just put in a request for a VCR to watch tapes. Whatever she wants she should have but you don't need a VCR to watch tapes. I have a roll of scotch tape on the desk and it is almost as boring to watch as TV. I went to the junk store (you may already know this) but for a VCR to work it must be attached to a TV. I bought a TV VCR combination for $3.00.

Management was delighted but I didn't understand she wanted it to be usable. I thought it was like a junk car. The pleasure is in having it, not driving it. She took it to a shop and had it repaired.

Now she wants a moat control. This is great. When we were building the house I wanted to install a moat complete with moat monsters and swans. If I get her a moat control then maybe she is finally going to let me build the moat.

Horses, Doctors and Odd Children

When I was young, people often said that I was an "odd" child. I never had a problem with that. Of course I was odd. My sister was born first, then my brother, then me and finally another brother. That makes me the 3rd child and 3 is odd in any math class. I did wonder why no one ever called my brothers "even" children. Like many other childhood nicknames, the "odd" stuck. A lady called me an "odd man" today. I had never met her before and I am still trying to figure out how she knew about my birth order.

I mis-located or dis-colated my good shoulder last week. Now, I not only walk with an odd lope, I am keeping my shoulder tucked in an odd angle. The first time I mis-located a shoulder I was in the 8th grade. We had just watched a Cowboy and Indian movie. In this politically correct world, I should say we had just watched a Purveyor of Animal Protein/Despoiler of the Environment and Native Culture (PAP/DE&NC) versus Native American movie.

In any case, the Indians were hanging onto their horse's manes and shooting arrows under the horse's neck so the PAP/DE&NC's could not shoot them. I was impressed. I had a bow and arrows, a horse (which had a neck), and saw no reason not to do the same.

In retrospect, there were several reasons I should not have attempted it. The most important being that the original Indians who did it did it for a living. They were professionals.

At that time, without the benefit of retrospection, I promptly went out, caught my horse, tied a rope halter on him, stripped to a loincloth, got my bow and arrows and found a suitable target. Both brothers being "even" children declined to participate.

There were a series of errors in my calculations. First, I discovered that contrary to my previous perceptions, Indians who rode horses bareback MUST have also worn underwear (I do not intend to discuss this). Secondly, my horse had not seen the movie and did not understand the process. Thirdly, Indian horses must have had a handle or super glue was really a Native American invention. And finally, that the ground in Southside Virginia is much harder than the ground on a movie set. All in all, it was a successful experiment except that my right shoulder was now two inches higher than the left. If I hadn't landed on my head I might have been seriously injured.

I have always suspected that my parents had worked out a volume discount arrangement with Dr. Bob, an ex-Army doctor. He had his own practice and did it all: delivered babies and set broken bones. He was a great doctor, but we boys hated to go to him. He treated all of us as if we were miniature soldiers.

"Well, Boy, what did you do stupid this time? Dislocated

your shoulder? I'll just yank it back in place." This time, he couldn't "yank" it back in place since the elbow was also broken. I left with 3-inch tape from navel to neck. I reported to my mother that "I had mis-located dis shoulder."

The next day I was back in his office in terrible pain, which was again diagnosed as stupidity. It appears I should NOT have gone riding after getting taped up. How was I supposed to know that? The biggest stupidity was admitting to falling rather than claiming to have been thrown. He removed the tape in his typical bedside manner, which involved cutting it down one side and gently pulling. The removal took almost one second. The local sawmill knocked off early for lunch that day and all of the volunteer firemen reported for duty. I'm certain Dr. Bob's hearing was damaged but not as much as my chance to ever have any chest hair.

Auctions, Projects And Service Trucks

I arrived at The Messenger office one day last week to find a note stuck in the door. It said. "I have heard that the Southside Messenger was started by Management in the hopes of getting you to clean up the junk in the yard." The note was signed "Curious in Meherrin."

Dear Curious, That is absolutely not true. Although Management does want me to clean up my collection of valuable and desirable vehicles, she did not attempt to do it this way. You have to understand that although my stuff, (which you so unkindly refer to as junk) does annoy her slightly, she is more opposed to what she calls my "projects." Projects are similar to stuff except that the monetary expenditure on them is much greater, as is the amount of time required to repair them and the amount of space they occupy.

It is possible that starting a newspaper qualifies as a project but I don't intend to bring that up. An example of a project is when she decided I needed a new (make that newer) service truck. Although there was nothing wrong with the VW hippie van I was driving as a work truck, she was in one of her "Averett Improvement Phases." She thought I would look more professional with a Standard Issue Service Van. I consider all vehicles to be trucks and if they cost more than $1000, that's just too much to pay to get from point A to Point B. Remember that fourth class driving beats first class walking anytime.

We went to the bank and made arrangements to borrow money for a van. Everything was approved, Management located a service truck that met her standards and sent me with a check to get it. It was a wonderful truck. Management has excellent taste. The only problem was the amount of money they wanted for it. I told the salesman that for that much money I expected a kitchen and two bathrooms. I left to calm my nerves before completing the transaction.

I then happened to stop at an auction. Now, if you know Management, you know she never allows me to attend an auction without an attendant and without my auction jacket. She bought me a beautiful Nehru type jacket for auctions. It is white and the only problem is that the sleeves are much too long. She wraps them around my back and ties them in the front. This usually makes it difficult for me to bid but she was so sweet to buy it for me I hate to complain. Since she didn't realize I might stop at an auction and thought I'd be coming straight home, she hadn't put me in my jacket AND hadn't sent an attendant.

The auction was for a house. It was the type that Real Estate Agents kindly call a "fixer upper." To those of us who are not in the real estate business "fixer upper" translates to "shack" or "slum." Unfortunately for Management this valuable residential real estate happened to be selling for less than a standard issue service truck. I also happened to have a check in my pocket for this amount. I was resisting the urge to bid when the auctioneer said, "This beautiful doublewide mobile home has a kitchen and two baths." Well, that was it for me. I was sent to get a service truck. This not only had more storage room, 8 wheels, AND a kitchen and a bath. I did forget to ask about a motor but Management hadn't said anything about that anyway.

Ten minutes later I was the proud owner of another project. Management was delighted as always. "At least you can't park it in the yard," she said. That was 8 years ago and I intend to complete the repairs some day- when I have the time.

Chores, Lists and Sequences

In most marriages there is a division of chores. Each spouse will make a list of things that the other needs to do. This is the way it works here. I have a list of things I need to do and Management has a list of things I need to do. According to Management, this is the way it should be. When we were first married, I mistakenly thought she would make a list for me and I would make a list for her. I had a lot to learn.

I am of the opinion that a list should not exceed one column on a business card. Management, on the other hand, uses legal pads and believes a list should contain everything remaining undone in the universe.

I believe a list should contain bite-sized nuggets so I can have the satisfaction of marking off items in this lifetime. She believes in efficient lists. My list will have items like: take trash to dump, dentist appt, write Rural Legends, pay bills, etc. Her list, although longer, has items such as: build house, fence farm, clean up yard, achieve world peace, stop contamination of the Chesapeake Bay watershed, pay off mortgage and so on. I intend to get to work on her list just as soon as I finish mine.

I have carried both lists for twenty years. I occasionally mark an item off of my list but so far no luck on hers. "Build a house" was the first one on her list.

This was a reasonable request. I would love to build her a house. First, I was distracted by poverty, then by the arrival of the children, then by more poverty. The wolf was at our door so long the children thought he was a family pet.

Throughout the poverty years, "Build House" waited patiently on my list. I finally started the house 12 years ago. Now her list has "finish house" on it.

My list has "pick up books in the living room." This may seem to you to be a simple chore. It is not. When you factor in the sequences it is impossible. I admit that I may have a few more books than some people, but none that I don't need. I would be happy to pick them up, but I have nowhere else to put them. First, I need to put shelves in the library. Before I can put the shelves in the library, I need to finish the walls. Before the walls, I need to finish the floor. Before I can finish the floor I need to move the stuff stored in the library to the living room. In order to move the stuff in the library, I have to get the books out of the living room floor. This is known as a revolving sequence.

Simple sequences are just as difficult. Management decreed that I should move a truck from the yard. You would think after five years she would have adjusted to the truck being there.

Move a truck sounds so simple- until the sequences start. To move a truck requires a chain unless the truck is running, which doesn't happen here. I need to find a chain. The chain is holding up the lawn mower so I can sharpen the blades. The sharpener is at a friend's house. If I'm going to his house, I need to take the trailer which has a load of posts for the fence, which I need to unload first. Three hours have passed. I am ready to move the truck. The truck has a flat tire, the sequences require I find an air tank, then remove the tire and take it to be repaired. The lug wrench is missing, as is the jack. These were hidden by the son as punishment for my father's tools that I lost. This is cosmic adjustment. "The sins of the children are passed to the fathers unto the 34 frustration" or something like that.

The truck never got moved. It's all a matter of sequences.

Telephones, Telemarketers And Clicks

I miss the telemarketers. If they hang up then I win. They are always so much fun to talk with.

"Mr. Jones, you have been selected to receive new windows for your home."

"That's great, I've always wanted windows. But won't *They* be able to see in?"

"Oh no, Mr. Jones, we also have a tinted window to protect your privacy."

"OK, just a minute." I put the phone down. "OK, I'm back, do you have one 24 by 36?"

"Mr. Jones, I'm certain we do, we will send a contractor who will..."

"Just a minute." (two minute wait this time) "Do you have one that is 32 by 40 with the curved top?"

"Yes sir, but we will send..."

"Just a minute" (5 minutes) "Sorry, I had to go to the attic. Do you have one----" I am interrupted.

"Mr. Jones, we need to send a contractor to measure them." She gets all of the necessary information. We make the appointment for the contractor.

"Wait a minute, I forgot to ask about the cannon ports. They will have cannon ports, won't they? I need the cannons in case *They* come by. Listen, do you think they can put some steel shutters, motion detectors and..."

CLICK!!!!

"Meester Jo nes, theeze iz Jose, calling I am to geeve you present of two day three night bacation in be-you-tee-ful Stan-tone, Ver-shin-yah resort."

It looks like I'm going to lose this one. This guy barely speaks English and is trying to make a living in a tough business. I can go look at a time-share and help him out. Halfway through the conversation I notice Jose's English has improved a little. Maybe I should have stayed an English teacher. I have to get in one good line or I will lose the game. I say very fast, "Look Jose, this is a scam, I don't believe in time shares and I don't believe in Stanton, Virginia. Have you ever really met anyone from Stanton Virginia, Its just a made up place."

I was expecting "No Comprende" but instead Jose said, "You don't believe in Stanton Virginia?"

"Jose, What happened to your accent?"

"Oh, I forgot the accent"

"Nice talking with you, Jose, you hang up first."
Click.

"Mister Jones, Have you considered what would happen to Mrs. Jones and the Jones children in the event of an accident or death?"

"I guess it would depend on what kind of accident they have."

"No, Mr. Jones, I mean in the unfortunate event that YOU meet with an accident."

"I guess they will come to the hospital, and If I expire they will come to the church, sing a few songs, say a few nice things, toss my ashes around, put my name on a rock, and say he had a wonderful time."

"Mr. Jones," (have you noticed how patient they are?) "I am talking about providing financial security for your family if you pass away." I think he means if I die but they don't like to say dead. "We offer a term life policy for as little as 25 dollars a month."

"Wait a minute, If I take out one of your policies on my wife and she dies then you will give me $50,000?"

"That's right and..."

I interrupt, "That woman is priceless; it would be an insult to insure her for a measly 50 grand."

"Mr. Jones if you feel like that about her then I'm sure you will want to provide for her if you pass away."

"If I were worth any more dead then she would take me out

in my sleep. I already have to sleep with one eye open just in case she realizes I'm worth more dead than alive. If I were worth any more dead, I would never be able to sleep again. If I can't sleep then I'll have an accident and die and then you will have to pay out all of that money when I haven't paid you any and don't you think it would be better for the children to grow with a father in the home than with all that money?"

Click.

Beaches, Sting Rays and Details

Management and I just returned from several days at the beach. Every year, my family has a reunion at Ocean Isle Beach in North Carolina. I always have a great time with the exception of the first time we went after Management and I were married. At the time my father (who didn't fish) had devised the plan to feed the family at the beach without major expense. He had a local lady make him a 100-yard gill net, which we would pull out into the ocean and catch fish on a large scale. (Management says I take after him in some ways.)

Well, on our first trip as newlyweds, we caught lots of skates, which are miniature versions of stingrays and manta rays. I had often heard that skates had poisonous spines, but I had researched the subject and discovered no reference to poison. We had just caught a skate and I was showing it to the kids when someone said, "Skates are poisonous." Just as I said, "No, they are not," the skate spiked me in the finger.

As it happened, there was an error in my research. There are dozens of kinds of skates and this particular species IS poisonous. The poison is similar to a bee sting and isn't considered to be dangerous. Another error in research here. Those of us who happen to be allergic to bee stings are equally allergic to skate poison. OOPS!!!!

So, after a quick trip to the Emergency Room and the usual shots to keep me from becoming permanently horizontal, the doctor gave me a handful of antihistamine with orders to take two tablets every four hours. Pills and orders in hand, Management and I returned to the beach house. It usually takes me a day to fully recover from a bee sting reaction, so I assumed this would be the same. Wrong again.

Management was a devoted wife and came up from the beach every four hours to give me my drugs. For four days I was semiconscious, only waking to take my two pills every four hours. In my more lucid moments, I was wondering if there was ever a case of skate fatality when the medication ran out and I began to improve. The problem was simple. The Doctor had given me sample packages of the medication. Each package contained two 25mg tablets. At least the top pack was 25mg, which is what he intended for me to take. The remaining packages were 100mg, two of which will make you unconscious.

There are several lessons here about poor research and

attention to details. I should have been more careful with the research, and Management should have used a larger dose if she was intending to collect on the life insurance. In any case, *The Brunswick Beacon* missed out on a great headline. All of us should have paid more attention to details.

Management Team Bank

"We'll Never Call You Stupid"

Truth, Children and The Management Team

I recently realized that I not only have Management to arrange my existence, she has a team of Assistants. I call them The Management Team.

They are a charming group of ladies. They show up at random in random places and either correct my behavior or help me out. Several members of the team work in our bank.

Management has strange theories regarding banking. One is that before I write a check, I should have enough money to cover the check. Another is that I should have deposit tickets. If I run out of deposit tickets, it means I have made lots of deposits. Lots of deposits mean lots of money so any checks I write should be OK, Right?

Allowing deposits and checks to race each other to the bank adds some excitement to their otherwise drab dull lives, not to mention adding excitement to mine when Management finds out one of the checks won the race.

Imagine being a check. Used once, kept for a few years and forgotten forever. They deserve at least one race. For some reason Management just can't comprehend my attempts at kindness to small bits of paper.

If she were not perfect then I might call this a small character flaw. Some of "The Team" works at the bank. They remember my account numbers, look up my balance and never call me stupid. (At least not where I can hear them.) What a great group of ladies.

Several of "The Team" works at local restaurants. I simply cannot buy a large serving of apple cobbler at one of them. Doll will say, "Jonesy, you know you got sugar and can't eat that." Sometimes I can negotiate if I promise to save half for later. At Dot's Place in Keysville, I get sugar free candy with my order. The Management Team takes care of me when I forget to take care of myself. This is one of the great things about living in Southside. Where else would I have people keeping me from being stupid without calling me stupid?

When our children were very young we attempted to teach them to tell the truth. One thing we felt strongly about was that parents should not be allowed to lie and then expect children to be truthful. This is especially important on the phone. How many times do we say, "Tell them I'm not here?" Not only did we think it was wrong, we both knew our children would say, "Daddy said to tell you he isn't home."

We arrived at the conclusion that, "He or she is unavailable, May I take a message?" is the only correct answer whether we were not home or just busy. We learned this early in our marriage when the bratlets were about five years old. We left them happily playing in the living room and were taking a nap.

Keep in mind that there are naps and then there are NAPS. Neither kind is a spectator sport and neither involves children.

We were attempting to take a nap and the children were coloring pictures and sliding them under the door. This is somewhat distracting. They were both coloring and both feeding pictures under the door. From our side it looked like a giant fax machine, not to mention the giggles from the other side. It is impossible to nap or NAP with this type of distraction.

I went out and gave them books and specific instructions. Later the phone rang and I heard, "Yes he is here, but he is unavailable" long silence. "Yes, she is here but she is unavailable too."

Long silence.

"They are locked in their room having personal time and we are supposed to read and not bother them unless someone is bleeding or the house is on fire."

I hope it was a telemarketer.

Truth, Fiction and the Wal-Mart Baby

When I was a young child, I discovered that telling the truth is easier than making something up.

I also learned that many people expect a lie and automatically disregard anything you say. This says something about them, but I don't have the energy to sort it out. When I was a teenager, I once arrived a little late to school. Well, actually I often arrived late but this time it was three or four hours. My explanation was, "The sun was shining, the birds were tweeting and I couldn't deal with a classroom." This was not acceptable. "Would you believe my car broke down?"

This was believable. My car did not break down, although with my vehicles this is a reasonable possibility. Please note, I did not say it did. I asked if they would believe it. They not only believed it, they excused the tardy.

Last Christmas, I had temporary custody of a delightful 18-month-old girl child. Our original children, who arrived as the by-product of a hobby, are now teenagers. When they were small, they went with me everywhere and I enjoyed the opportunity to warp developing young minds. I taught them Ray Stevens, Kipling, Dr. Seuss and Shakespeare. They helped me milk goats, and we built a volcano that actually erupted. Not with vinegar and soda but with fire and ashes. Management still thinks volcanoes should be an outside hobby (if it had erupted another foot higher, inside would have been outside). We caught snakes.

But back to my Wal-Mart baby. Her mother was an acquaintance of Management and I first met the child at Wal-Mart. Several months later the mother had to make a trip out of the country and asked us to keep Grace. Not being able to resist another young mind to warp, I jumped at the chance. Her mother brought her over and I could immediately see something had to be done about her clothes. What she had just wouldn't do. The poor child needed real clothes. As soon as her mother left we went to the Good Will store and got her some real clothes. Frilly dresses and white fluffy coats just aren't conducive to my life style. She looked like a real Jones in her new, used denim and plaid.

We then stopped for coffee at a local restaurant. In response to, "Where did you get the baby," I answered, "I found her at Wal-Mart." Most people laughed but a few demanded more information.

I said, "I found her at Wal-Mart," which was true. I then pointed out that there are babies in carts all over Wal-Mart, many unattended like someone took them off of a shelf, put them in a cart and then changed their minds. Also true. I pointed out that babies are everywhere in all sizes, shapes, and colors. Also true. I added that when you go through a check out line with a baby they only charge you for the stuff in the cart but never the baby. More truth.

Several people demanded to know whose she was. "Mine for now," Also true. How long will I have her? "Until she leaves." "When will that be?" "I don't know, the first ones are still around and it's been 17 years." Are these people frustrated dropouts from law school?

I'm sticking with the truth. She didn't come with a birth certificate. I found her at Wal-Mart. And she was mine until she left.

Several of these people need to get a life. One went to see my mother. Keep in mind that this person hadn't been to see Mrs. J. for 20 years. Suddenly, she felt the need to visit her. During the visit she casually asked, "Whose baby is Averett keeping?" Mrs. J replied, "He told me he found her at Wal-Mart and I believe him."

Another "inquiring mind" cornered the daughter and demanded an answer. She responded, "She is the love child of an actress who is touring Europe and vacationing in the Isle de Canaris and Dad is keeping her until she returns."

The inquisitor stalked off complaining, "Why can't y'all tell the truth?" It was the truth.

The Light at the End of the Tunnel

Management frequently tells me she wants to see the light at the end of the tunnel. I can tell her from personal experience that it isn't all it's cracked up to be. I have seen the light twice.

Once was just after I discovered I was allergic to bee stings. I was climbing a tree to get a swarm of bees. Now it is a fact that a swarm of bees is gentle and easy to handle. It also happens to be a fact that occasionally honeybees build a hive hanging on the limb of a tree. This looks just like a swarm but actually has a honeycomb inside. Bees are very protective of a hive, that's their job. I was wearing protective gear, which consisted of shorts and a tee shirt. The bees resented my attempts to move them into row housing which, in retrospect, was fair. Had I not fallen from the tree I might have been hurt. As it was, I escaped with only several hundred stings.

There are many theories on the treatment of bee stings. Sanford, the older man with me, believed in Mercurochrome. He whipped a bottle of it from his pocket and proceeded to dab it on.

Several hundred stings on a 150lb body pretty well covers the whole thing. I immediately knew something was wrong. I drove to Dr. Bob's office, staggered in, said "bee stings" and passed out. I saw a long tunnel with a light at the end. I was watching Dr. Bob and the nurses frantically working one me. It was fascinating. They were excited and I was asleep.

There is sufficient evidence that I survived but from then on Dr. Bob made it his mission to tell me I was stupid for keeping bees when I was allergic to them. Although, to be fair, he only brought it up when he had to give me a shot for a reaction to them.

30 years ago, I was in Brainerd, Tennessee, which is a suburb of Chattanooga. We decided to go into Chatty for some reason or the other. Incidentally, some reason or the other usually means something I wouldn't want my parents to know, or women. In any case, just as we reached the city limits we heard a loud crash and everything stopped. For a few minutes there was absolute silence, then it sounded like thousands of trumpets blowing. I thought, "This is it."

As I stepped from the car, I heard my friend saying, "Jones, don't go." I started walking toward a bright light. The sounds of trumpets continued and my friend's voice faded. After several hundred feet, I could see a man standing in the center of a circle of light. I considered going back but was drawn to the light. As I got even closer I could see him motioning me to come faster.

This did not have the desired effect. I was not ready to meet this man. As I got closer, I could see his face and was surprised to see that he didn't appear to be much older than I. You may have expected for him to have a peaceful expression but to me he looked stern. As I came closer, the trumpets stopped and he spoke. "Boy, you in a heap of trouble, Where you from?"

I expected better grammar. He just waited for me to answer. As you may know, there is a certain pride in all Virginians. When you ask one where he is from, he will say Virginia. He will say this in North Carolina, Texas, Mexico, Europe and on Mars. This didn't seem appropriate this time, so I responded, "Earth."

He didn't seem to like this answer. "Boy, I'm gonna take you somewhere you won't like."

I remembered I had a date later and needed to get back to school so I apologized. "Boy" he said, "You kinda dumb, you been blocking the East Ridge Tunnel for half an hour. Don't you know when your car breaks down in a tunnel you are supposed to remain with your car?"

Everything worked out fine. The State Policeman was a fine man. The car was towed, I got back to school in time and the officer didn't take me to jail.

So much for the light at the end of the tunnel.

Reindeer, Frosty and Christmas Cheer

I sometimes wake up in the middle of the night to ponder things. Since it is almost Christmas, I ponder Christmassy things. I have learned to ponder quietly and without requesting any input from Management. Years ago, I woke her up to ask her how many legs Frosty the Snowman had. Sometimes I worry about her. "Do you know what time it is?" she asked.

Of course I did. It was 3:22 AM o'clock in the morning. "You just woke me up to ask me that." That was obvious. She said "two" and went back to sleep. I wouldn't have been pondering it if he had two legs. I got up, found a record of the song and spent several hours trying to get the "thumpty, thump, thump, thumpty thump" cadence. It just can't be done, walking or running.

It turns out the answer is obvious. Frosty didn't have any legs. Just that round ball at the bottom like most snowmen. He bounced. Listen to the song again. "Thumpty, thump thump, thumpty thump. Look at Frosty go." Management says I am the only person in the universe concerned by this. Of course I'm concerned. This is another case of politically correct gone wrong. Why would anyone force a snowman to have legs? People have legs, animals have legs, tables have legs, chairs have legs, Yeti and Abominable Snowmen have legs but standard issue snowmen have a ball on the bottom.

Another Christmas concern is the names of Santa's reindeer. The eight tiny reindeer were born in 1921 in Troy, NY. Prior to that Santa only had one Reindeer or he rode a horse. You know the poem. "Now, Dasher! Now, Dancer! Now, Prancer and Vixen! On, Comet, On, Cupid, on Donder and Blitzen!" Notice there is no Rudolph. He didn't arrive until 1939. So here's my concern. They all have typical names except Donder and Blitzen, which mean Thunder and Lightning in several languages. I prefer to think more highly of old Santa than that. Did he say, "OOPS, I've run out of English names, I guess I'll go Dutch?"

Nobody names like that, not even me. Have you ever seen a family that named their children or pets, Fred, Bob, Sally, Alice and Plutarch Loinfruit? This is something to ponder. Who named Donder and Blitzen?

After years of pondering this and some serious research, I finally have the answer. Clement Moore, the alleged author of "The Night Before Christmas," named Donder and Blitzen. He just didn't write the rest of the poem.

My third Christmas ponder-able is Christmas Cheer. In Southside we all know what a cheer is. You sit in a cheer at the table eating Christmas dinner. I don't know what kind of rich folks have a set of cheers just for Christmas. Maybe a plate with some holly berries painted on it, but not cheers. Where would you keep them for the rest of the year?

Wait, words have two meanings in Southside. **Christmas Cheer refers to Rot Cheer as opposed to yonder.** We're not going over yonder to visit the children this year. We are going to celebrate Christmas cheer.

This year I did my Christmas shopping early. I bought everybody batteries. I found a huge box of batteries on eBay. Some people will get double A's; some C cell and some will get D's. I even have some of the itty bitty triple A's and 9 volt. I already know to whom I'm going to give the D cells. I have a friend who constantly talks about how much he likes double D's. I'll give him an even dozen. He should be happy all year. I'm so proud of me. This is the first time I've done my shopping early. I hope everyone likes the batteries.

I even printed some nice cards that say:

MERRY CHRISTMAS
I hope you enjoy the batteries.
(Gift not included.)